Landscapes of The Rockies

Text by
Eileen Coppola

CRESCENT BOOKS
NEW YORK

CLB 1257
© 1985 Illustrations Colour Library Books and Parks Canada.
© 1985 Text: Colour Library Books Ltd., Guildford, Surrey, England.
Text filmsetting by Acesetters Ltd., Richmond, Surrey, England.
All rights reserved.
Published 1985 by Crescent Books, distributed by Crown Publishers, Inc.
Printed in Spain.
ISBN 0 517 460750
h g f e d c b a

The Rocky Mountains – magnificent, majestic, spectacularly beautiful – there just aren't enough grand adjectives to describe them adequately. A land of snow-capped peaks, superb wilderness and teeming wildlife, where the Continental Divide separates the cascading waters that flow westward to the Pacific from those that head eastward to the Atlantic, the Rockies have been an ancient and sacred home to generations of Indians and a source of fascination to those who came later, lured there by the search for adventure, the promise of easy wealth or simply by the pursuit of a dream.

Travel through the Rockies and you will stand time and time again, like millions before you, hypnotized, amazed and bewitched by their sheer splendor and drama. There is something magnetic and mystical about the region, something that gets inside you and makes you want to make it a part of you. Whether it is the grandeur of the desolation, the vastness of the region or the magnificent palette of color seducing the eye that excites your senses, you will never forget the experience – or the sense of tranquility that comes from being at one with nature at her most awesome.

The dazzling scenery of the Rocky Mountains offers, as that of few other places in the world, some of those exquisite moments when silence and solitude are not unwelcome... moments like those when the first rays of the early morning sun bathe the mountain peaks in pale pink flesh-tones, or when you come upon a sunny grove of aspen trees or flowering columbine and goldbloom saxifrage bursting with color, or the breathtaking beauty of tall, slim pines reflected in the still waters of a sparkling lake where birds flit and chatter.

And the taste of sweet water from a mountain stream is something you'll never forget. Nor will you forget the thrill of skiing down powdered slopes, with that feeling of freedom that wide-open space gives you – the wind on your face, the air crisp and clear. These are moments that will take your breath away and stay in your heart forever.

And if you're lucky enough to see one, another magnificent spectacle in the mountains is a thunderstorm (view it at a safe distance, though, since the warm air near a human body is an excellent conductor of electricity). Great billowy clouds roll over and over, the margins of the gigantic mass thin and gray, the blue, luminous sky surrounding the whole form. Sometimes, streaks of sunlight appear through the clouds, creating dazzling rainbows and lighting the landscape below. Violent winds erupt, uprooting trees and thrashing those strong enough to resist being blown away. Lightning crackles across the sky and ear-splitting roars of thunder roll along the mountains, creating a wild and fearsome setting that, while beautiful to watch, instills a wholehearted respect for the powers of nature!

The Rocky Mountains have long captivated men's imaginations and fired their hearts. Their sheer ruggedness and vastness presents a challenge to conquer them – just because they're there. The largest mountain system in North America, the Rockies stretch over 3,000 miles through the United States and Canada, reaching a width of about 3,550 miles in some locations. In the U.S., the varied and never tiresome landscape of the Rockies spreads across some 864,000 square miles through Colorado, Wyoming, Montana, Idaho, Utah, Nevada, Arizona and New Mexico – the so-called "Mountain States" – painting the canvas with barren, sun-drenched plateaus, soaring, ice-capped peaks, canyons that plunge to incredible depths, glacial areas, salt flats and sizzling deserts. As if that's not enough for any lover of nature, there are also rolling meadows, jewel-like lakes, phenomenal geysers and hot springs, and thundering waterfalls.

Wildlife abounds in the Rocky Mountains, which are a sportsman's heaven in the hunting season. Bears, elk, deer, minks, porcupines, mountain lions and a host of other animals live on the higher forested slopes, while coyotes, moose, muskrats and chipmunks make their homes in the grassy valleys between the mountains.

The Rockies also boast the swiftest mammal on the continent – the pronghorn, a distant relative of the deer family. Wintering in the low-lying canyons, it moves to the high plains in the summer, its keen eyes able to spot a predator as soon as it appears on the horizon.

The pronghorn uses the white patch on its rump to signal to other members of the herd. When the animal becomes frightened, its muscles contract so that the white hairs of the patch rise and it flashes in the sun. At the same time, the pronghorn emits a musky odor as a warning. The combination enables it to communicate danger to the rest of the herd even though they are widely scattered over the plains.

Goats and bighorn sheep live above the timberline (beyond which trees are unable to grow because of the icy temperatures). The Rocky Mountain goat (which is not a true goat, but more related to the antelope) is a lover of solitude. The male of the species prefers to be alone most of the year, only becoming gregarious during the November mating season! But this preference for living high and remote among the rocks is mainly a protection against predators, who will not venture there.

An interesting biological feature enabling the mountain goat to scale precarious heights lies in the construction of its hooves, which have sharp, hard rims for cutting into ice, thick balls of flesh that provide traction on the most slippery of surfaces and spaces between the two that form suction cups, giving the animal a firm grip on the ground and an air of self-possessed confidence on the most precipitous of overhangs.

Autumn provides an annual mountain delicacy for summer wildlife visitors to the peaks as they migrate down the slopes. Deer, bears, coyotes, birds and rodents re-entering the timberline feast on the succulent blueberries that ripen in the fall. (In a lean winter, if the pickings are slim and it is not able to fell a mule deer or land other prey such as rodents or rabbits, a coyote will not turn its nose up at juniper berries or wild rosehips, thus sustaining itself on more delicate fare than usual.)

Though the Rockies are a paradise for wildlife fanciers, bird lovers and fishermen will find themselves in heaven too (especially if the latter fancy rainbow trout). Sheep and cattle ranching are sustained by rich grazing lands, and this plentiful region also yields timber and minerals such as gold, silver, copper, zinc and uranium – supplying lucrative resources to both the lumber and mining industries.

Tourists flock here by the million each year – to see the sights, to ski, swim, hike, camp, ride the rapids, visit a dude ranch, or just to enjoy the serenity and inexhaustible beauty of the area and escape from the pressures of daily living.

For above all, the Rocky Mountains have retained their wilderness aura, which endures despite man's excesses and his continual ravaging of the land without replenishing what he takes.

Keeping their essential isolation, the mountains remain wild, offering a gift with which to live in harmony; something the Indians understood and respected, living as they did in a culture created by and of the mountains. When the white man moved compulsively to civilize and bend the land to his will, he destroyed in the process much of what had so enticed him.

In the early dawn of prehistoric times, millions – perhaps a billion – of years ago, most of what is now the Western United States was covered by a vast sea. Then, pressure and heat from within the earth created first gentle tremors, then a dramatic upheaval that forced the Ancestral Rockies up above the waters.

But even as this mountain building was taking place, wind and water were eroding the peaks, pushing sand, silt and gravel back into the surrounding area. By about 200 million years ago, the Ancestral Rockies had completely worn away, and the inland sea had again returned.

In a series of geological changes, deserts were built and swampy lowlands formed over most of the Mountain States, creating a tropical climate in which dinosaurs thrived. In time, rock debris was carried into the swamps from low, bordering hills that eventually solidified into sedimentary rock, but over millions of years these too were worn away into the sea. And always, heat and pressure lay in the innards of the earth, seeking an outlet.

And eventually it came, in the significant geological development that geologists call the Laramide Revolution. Occurring about 160 million years ago and lasting for 100 million years, the Laramide Revolution prepared the base for the Rockies. During this period, the crust of the earth, weakened and strained by the weight of water and silt, gave way to internally-generated pressures, its surface buckling and folding. New mountain ranges lifted from the sea, raising the entire land area significantly and altering the balance between land and water, foretelling the sea's eventual disappearance.

During the 60 million years following the Laramide Revolution, several major forces structured the Rocky Mountains and their present grandeur: during what must have been a period of awesome fireworks, volcanic activity shaped mountains and plateaus; the pressures of a great squeeze wrinkled and pinched the Rockies upward into high folds, lifting their granite core; great masses of earth slipped along lines of weakness, or faults, in the earth's crust, forming fault-block mountains.

And then, some 2 million years ago, the great sculptors of the Rocky Mountains, the mighty and magnificent blue-veined glaciers, moved slowly and surely to carve and shape the mountains, smoothing craggy peaks and rounding out valleys, pushing before them the piles of rock and earth called moraines, which came to rest where melting finally stopped their downward thrust.

The story of the building up and tearing down of the mountains is an ongoing saga. Glaciers continue to grind their way down the high mountain slopes, and volcanic activity continues to shape and alter the landscape. In Yellowstone National Park's Mammoth Hot Springs, for instance, once abundant evergreens are no longer able to thrive because of the hot-spring water that surges around them. As they have for billions of years, the forces of nature continue their work of erosion and replenishment, furthering the geological process by re-creating the re-designing a landscape of never-ceasing wonder.

The first civilizations to appear on the Rocky Mountain landscapes were those of the Indians, long before the explorers and trappers and miners and ranchmen had even thought of venturing into the region. The Indians' ancestors, primitive hunters of Mongolian stock, had come to North

America from Asia thousands of years before. The absorption of much of the earth's waters by ice had caused submerged land to appear at that time, and a land bridge about 300 miles wide linked Siberia with Alaska, enabling these early hunters to pursue their prey – Ice Age mammals like the big-horned bison and the hairy mammoth – as they grazed along the Bering Land Bridge and down into North America.

The nomads' migration lasted about 3,000 years, during which time some of these hunters settled in the high plains east of the Rocky Mountains, while others settled the Great Basin and Colorado plateaus between the mountains and the Sierra Nevada.

Those living in the westerly regions subsisted on the small game and plants native to this relatively dry area, while the plains dwellers continued to hunt big game, pursuing the easily-spotted herds on foot and driving the animals over cliffs or surrounding them and then killing them with stone-tipped spears. These hunting expeditions provided them with the necessities of life, the animal carcasses and hides furnishing food, clothing, shelter and tools fashioned from bone and sinew. When the glaciers began to recede about 10,000 years ago, many of the hunters' big prey died out.

Forced by necessity to change their way of life, the big game hunters developed a whole new set of habits and created the Desert Culture. A society dependent on hunting now learned to use all of the various food resources offered by their rigorous climate – combing the land for smaller animals like rabbit and antelope, for plants, berries, nuts, fish and even reptiles and locusts (considered a delicacy). They learned a new mobility as well, following concentrations of plants and animals as the seasons and the rains dictated. Their tools and implements grew more sophisticated, and they wove some of the world's earliest known basketry from locally-available grasses.

During the time between the retreat of the glaciers and the arrival of the white man on the continent, three distinctive Indian cultures developed on the Rocky Mountain region: Great Basin and Colorado Plateau Indians; Plains Indians; and those of the Desert Culture.

The Plains Indians added farming to their hunting-and-gathering economy and lived a semi-sedentary life. The Pueblo Indians learned to grow maize and to irrigate the land. They became accomplished potters and basketmakers and built permanent adobe homes. Now known as the Anasazi, or "Ancient Ones," the Pueblo Indians at first built pit houses and over the next hundred years moved above ground, creating many-tiered villages built into cliff recesses or on top of mesas. Theirs was a cohesive society centered round a complex religion that involved all members of the community in elaborate ceremonies. One large building – the Great Kiva – was set aside strictly for religious and ceremonial purposes.

No one knows exactly what happened to the Pueblo Indians,

but sometime in the 14th century they abandoned their highly developed way of life and their cliff dwellings and went out into the canyons and the desert, some of them taking up the Desert Culture once again. It is possible that a combination of drought, raids by hostile Navajos and Apaches, and internal feuding caused the break-up of this great society.

The society of the Desert Culture peoples – known as the Shoshoneans, a collective name for the Ute, Shoshone, Gosiute and other tribes that lived in Utah, Colorado and Wyoming – was simple and seemingly unencumbered by the headaches that accompany more sophisticated societies. Men and women shared the labor; both cared for the children; no one in the family had final authority over the others, but the wisest members offered advice. Both men and women often had several spouses. Because they were nomads, and the land belonged to no one in particular, anyone could go anywhere in search of food. They had no priests and no aristocrats. Those who had especially powerful dreams became shamans, whose duty was to cure people and who were considered especialy wise. Warfare was infrequent and impractical, since these Indians recognized few territorial rights and had no system that rewarded military valor.

The Plains Indians, on the other hand, had warrior societies and were warlike tribes, eager to undertake dangerous enterprises to gain wealth and prestige. Fond of ceremony, they usually performed an important ritual, the Sun Dance, before going out to hunt or to raid. A participant in the Sun Dance would first go without food or water, then dance around a sacred pole for days, sometimes suspending himself from the pole by skewers thrust into his flesh that would tear loose as he danced. This self-mortification was intended to induce powerful visions that would guide the warrior in his hunting or raiding mission. To the Plains Indian aggressiveness, daring and competition for status were a way of life, and combat was essential to it.

As the white man pushed his way into Indian territory, taking their land and forcing them further and further westward, the rivalry for land and the goods offered by the new arrivals greatly increased among tribes. Armed and mounted, the Indians struggled in earnest to hold onto their land, fighting against each other and against the white man. Those who tried to adapt to the white man's way soon found that their new life of wealth from bartering and trading was dependent upon the white man for its continued existence.

In time, the white presence altered the Indians' way of life profoundly and irreversibly, eradicating the buffalo herds on which many were dependent, almost eliminating the beaver population in a frenzy of trapping, and spreading diseases such as measles and smallpox, which took an enormous toll amongst the Indians. The white man's whiskey, which he used as a cheap trade for furs and encouraged the Indians to drink, also had disastrous effects.

In his westward expansion and the fulfillment of Manifest

Destiny, the frontiersman had no notion of peaceful co-existence with the Indian. He was an obstacle in the path of progress and was to be gotten rid of, regardless of how valiantly he fought and how many times he compromised and agreed to the terms of the white man's treaties.

Battle upon battle was fought, slaughter and massacre occurred on both sides time and time again. The Indian was cheated and betrayed over and over, treated without respect or honor, his rightful lands taken from him and his tribes relegated to reservations on inferior land.

Nor was he allowed to escape to freedom: in 1877, U.S. troops pursued Chief Joseph and his Nez Percé Indians as he led them in a retreat to Canada through Idaho and Montana. After a trek of some 1,300 miles, the Indians (who had been moved from their homeland in the Wallowa Valley of Oregon and were resisting being moved to a smaller reservation) surrendered following several small battles and a two-day battle at Big Hole, in Montana. They were captured only 40 miles from the Canadian border.

The following year, they were sent to the Indian Territory in what is now Oklahoma.

When Chief Joseph died in 1904, it was said to be from a "broken heart," having watched the suffering of his people and the loss of all that meant life to them.

The first Europeans to make their way to the Rocky Mountains were Spanish explorers, drawn to this new land by a desire for adventure and wealth. Tales of opulent cities, of a land of gold and silver, spurred them on, and dreams of easy riches that lay just around the next corner fired them with dogged determination.

One of the earliest fortune hunters was Coronado, who is believed to have entered the Colorado territory in 1540 with an entourage of 400 men – Spanish conquistadors in elaborate plumes and shining armor. They brought with them an impressive assemblage of horses, pack animals, goat and sheep herds and slaves and, of course, the priests that accompanied every Spanish expedition. Part of their mission was to introduce "civilization" and "religion" to the Indians. They could not have known that the most valuable thing Spain would introduce to the Indians was the horse, which was unknown in North America until the arrival of Spanish explorers on the continent.

These conquistadors came in search of the famed Seven Cities of Cibolla, legendary places laden with emeralds and other precious stones, with gold and silver and treasure there for the taking. When they found Cibolla, their dreams were dashed to the ground. This village and surrounding villages had some precious stones, but they were not cities of gold and silver. Instead, the Spaniards found many-tiered villages of adobe that were a far cry from their expectations.

Unwilling to admit defeat, and certain that the fabled wealth existed somewhere, they listened eagerly to the tales of an Indian they called "El Turko," who must have had a tongue of gold, judging from his ability to beguile them with stories of the fabulous city of Quivira. As El Turko spun his yarn of the incomparable Quivira, Coronado and his men were seized with a vision of a city whose streets were paved with gold; whose palace of rarest marble was reflected in the blue waters of a nearby lake – a city of wealth beyond their wildest dreams, where royal canoes sported golden oarlocks and where golden bells chimed hypnoticaly in the gentle breezes. (If it sounds like El Turko's version of Shangri-La, it was!)

The expedition headed north, bound and determined for glory and riches. Hundreds of miles later, dusty, dirty and tired, the caravan found itself on the site where Quivira was supposed to be. Instead of a city of splendor, they found a desolate spot in Kansas.

Why had the Indian lied? No one knows. But there are lots of opinions and conjectures about El Turko's behavior: that he planned to steal away from the Spaniards, carrying all the loot he could manage; that he planned to lead them into ambush; or that he was trying to get them as far as possible from the Pueblo Indians whose villages they had entered. Whatever the Indian's reasons, Coronado was so angry upon learning of the deception that he strangled El Turko in his sleep. The golden tongue would tell no more tales.

The Spanish visitors continued to come to the shining mountains for more than 200 years – explorers such as De Soto, de Vaca, Rivera Oñate and Escalante. And, indeed, many of them found the precious ores that had eluded their predecessors.

Although Spain generally contented herself with exploration on the fringe of the Rockies, some of these expeditions also made attempts to find easy routes through the mountain barrier, coming away with at least marginal impressions of the interior.

Some of those who came to look stayed on, bringing their rich Spanish heritage to a new culture. One of the cities they founded was Santa Fe, New Mexico, the nation's oldest capital city (1610), a place softened by the mellow patina of antiquity, where you can see the rich intermingling of Indian, Spanish and American cultures.

In 1762, France had ceded Louisiana to Spain in a treaty following the Seven Years' War – to compensate for Spanish losses and also to prevent Great Britain from acquiring Louisiana as well as Canada at the peace conference. In 1800, Napoleon forced Spain to return Louisiana in the Treaty of San Ildefonso – part of his plan to restore the French Empire in North America.

Continuing that effort, he assembled two armies – he sent one to San Domingo in 1802 to overthrow Toussaint L'Ouverture, the island's dictator, and the other, assembled in secret, was intended to secure Louisiana against the British, with whom war was on the imminent horizon.

The strategy was that the troops in San Domingo would reinforce the Louisiana army once they had completed their mission on the island. But even a great military genius like Napoleon was to learn that the best laid plans of mice and men go awry. Though the French army in San Domingo did capture L'Ouverture, it was wiped out by yellow fever, and the Louisiana regiment, which then had to be sent to San Domingo, didn't fare much better, succumbing both to yellow fever and to fierce guerrilla activity.

Seeing that he had to abandon his plan of attacking Great Britain via the Western Hemisphere, Napoleon revised his strategy with plans for an attack by way of Germany and the English Channel. Since it was clear to him that Great Britain would seize Louisiana when war broke out, he determined to sell Louisiana to the United States – thus robbing the English of the opportunity for an enormous increase in power and wealth.

From the American standpoint, France's upcoming possession of Louisiana was a threat to its security, for this fledgling country would be up against the greatest military power of the time. Then, in 1802, with the transfer of Louisiana by Spain to France still pending, Spain withdrew from the Americans the right of deposit at New Orleans – cargo could no longer be trans-shipped from river boats to ocean-going vessels without customs or excise fees. Commerce in that area would be crippled and it was thought that when France took possession of Louisiana the entire Mississippi would remain closed to American trade. With access to the Mississippi and the Gulf of Mexico cut off, the economy of the West would be strangled.

Early in the game, when the American President, Thomas Jefferson, first learned of the pending cession of Louisiana to France, he instructed the American Minister to France, Robert R. Livingston, to negotiate for the purchase of New Orleans or for the right of deposit. The French Foreign Minister, Talleyrand, seemed to turn a deaf ear, but by October of 1802, when the Spanish closed the Mississippi, it was evident that Napoleon's San Domingo strategy had turned into a fiasco and that Talleyrand's attitude might change.

The situation was an extremely sensitive one. Since the closure of the river, there was the possibility that hot-headed Westerners might take it upon themselves to open the Mississippi and take New Orleans, exposing the U.S. to the danger of war with Spain and possible attack by France or Great Britain.

A believer in the value of diplomacy, Jefferson appointed James Monroe Minister Extraordinary and Plenipotentiary and sent him to Paris to negotiate American rights in the Mississippi. By the time Monroe arrived in France in 1803, Napoleon had already made up his mind to sell Louisiana to the United States, and Monroe, who had been commissioned to buy a city of some 7,000 inhabitants, found his colleague Robert Livingston negotiating for the purchase of an area 43,000 miles greater than the area of the United States at the time of the purchase! The 909,000 square mile area cost approximately 4 cents an acre.

Although Jefferson probably did not expect to acquire all of Louisiana at this time, he was well aware of American expansion west of the Mississippi and of the sovereignty that was sure to follow. In a secret message to Congress dated January 18, 1803, five days after Monroe's appointment, Jefferson announced his intention of sending an expedition to explore a water route for American commerce across the territory of a foreign power. It is not unlikely that he foresaw that the territory would eventually become U.S. territory.

While the expedition was to be for scientific exploration and to serve as an inland probe for a Northwest Passage to the Orient, Jefferson's foresight had in mind the Canadian fur trade, the lucrative trade in sea otter and China goods, and the Columbia River, where the U.S. had a fragile claim on Oregon through Captain Robert Gray's discovery of the Columbia's mouth in 1792.

The expedition was commanded by Captain Meriwether Lewis and by Captain William Clark. In 1803, Lewis was twenty-nine years old and Clark was thirty-three, both of them young and vigorous and a match for the rugged adventure they were about to undertake.

Lewis was trained in botany, zoology and celestial navigation. He was the scientific specialist, with a speculative mind, introverted and mercurial and subject to fits of anger and depression. Clark was the engineer, the geographer and the master of frontier crafts. He had skill in dealing with Indians and was the superior riverman of the two. He was extroverted and even-tempered. Both men were intellectually distinguished, and that element was greatly responsible for the success of the expedition.

Lewis was a friend of the Jefferson family and served as Jefferson's private secretary for two years, so he was well aware of the President's interest in exploration of the Missouri River and the lands west of its source. Particularly suited to undertake such an expedition because of his experience of military command and wilderness life, Lewis found the undertaking to be what he called "a darling project of my heart."

Jefferson's instructions to Lewis were very specific: "The object of your mission is to explore the Missouri River, such principal stream of it, as, by it's (sic) course and communication with the waters of the Pacific Ocean, may offer the most direct and practicable water communication across the continent, for the purposes of commerce." Jefferson wanted copious notes made on all that the expedition observed and encountered, and advised Lewis to make several copies of his notes against the possibility of loss, even going so far as to suggest that one copy of the notes be made on "the paper of the birch, as less liable to injury from damp than common paper."

The discovery of a water route across North America would

be of priceless value – the trip to the coast would be shortened, costs would be cut drastically and hazards would be virtually eliminated, because such a route would be protected against privateers, blockades and navies. Moreover, as mentioned before, it would give the U.S. a chance to compete for the Canadian fur trade by providing access to the beaver country.

While the Rockies had been crossed in 1793 by the Canadian Alexander Mackenzie, that was far to the north and there was still only a vague notion of how extensive and how wide they might be. And the kind of obstacle they represented to transporting freight by water was unknown.

The Lewis and Clark expedition was gone for three years, voyaging up the Missouri River, across the Rockies and down to the coast at the mouth of the Columbia River. The difficulty of the journey, the dangers the party experienced throughout in their encounter with a wilderness so rugged cannot be overstated. Nothing in their past wilderness experience had prepared them for it, and radically different techniques were needed in order to survive.

The leadership and strict discipline of Lewis and Clark in commanding their party of fourteen soldiers, seven hunters and Clark's black slave, York, is to be credited for the expedition's smooth and efficient progress. Only one death occurred – that of Sargeant Charles Floyd, who was stricken with a ruptured appendix – although Lewis was shot in the leg by a one-eyed hunter who mistook him for a bear! The only momentary lapse in the party's morale occurred in the Bitterroot Mountains of Montana, when the food supply failed.

The confidence exhibited by these pathfinders in the face of the unknown is absolutely remarkable. Confronted not only with the Rockies, but with treacherous river waters, high plains and plateaus, tremendous forests and bitter winter cold, grizzly bears and sometimes-hostile Indians, they exhibited an intrepid courage and daring that is a part of the wilderness spirit.

They got all the adventure they could want and more, plus a glimpse of some of the most magnificent wilderness in the world at its preternatural best. In one of his journal entries, Lewis captures a scene that was to become more and more rare: "...this senery already rich pleasing and beautiful was still farther hightened by immence herds of Buffaloe, deer Elk and Antelopes which we saw in every direction feeding on the hills and plains. I do not think I exagerate when I estimate the number of Buffaloe which could be compre(hend)ed at one view to amount to 3000." (Spellings, punctuation and capitalizations are his.)

In their dealings with Indians, Lewis and Clark exhibited respect, fairness, courage and firmness. During a tense, four-day encounter with Teton Sioux, when any show of fear or weakness or any lapse of vigilance whould have been disastrous in the face of the Indians' bullying, blustering and threatening tactics, they showed that their nerve did not fail and that they were not afraid. The message spread that a new breed of white men that could not be scared or bullied had come to the upper Missouri.

When the party wintered with the Mandan Indians in North Dakota, they were joined by a French trader, Charbonneau, and his Shoshone wife, Sacajawea, then perhaps only sixteen years old. Lewis' journal entry for February 11, 1805 records that Sacajawea underwent a slow and painful labor in giving birth to her first child. At the suggestion of one of his men, who said he had never seen the remedy fail, Lewis broke two rings of the rattle of a snake into small pieces, mixed them with water and administered this less than delectable potion to Sacajawea to hasten the child's birth. It worked! And she delivered a fine, healthy boy shortly after. But Lewis reserved judgement: "Whether this medicine was truly the cause or not I shall not undertake to determine, but I was informed that she had not taken it more than ten minutes before she brought forth."

Finding itself unable to continue the journey by boat because of the terrain and shallow river waters, the expedition hoped to negotiate with the Snake Indians, the Shoshones, for horses so that it could go on by land for whatever distance was required. Sacajawea was especially helpful at this point as she served as an interpreter and goodwill ambassador with the already-friendly Shoshones.

In what sounds like the script of a grade-B movie, Sacajawea discovered the Snake Chief to be her long-lost brother and was reunited with him and with her people, from whom she had been taken captive by other Indians.

The Lewis and Clark expedition ended the search for the Northwest Passage, proving as it did that a commercially practicable water route to the Pacific did not exist, and brought a chapter of history to a close. But it was invaluable in turning the unknown into a reality, providing the first knowledge of the American West – a far, enigmatic country that had never been described – and making it something tangible with which the mind could deal... a land of lakes and rivers, of mountains, plateaus, valleys, flora and fauna, and of Indian tribes; and a land whose treasury of beaver beckoned.

They were called the mountain men – the men who trailed the beaver. They were the map-makers of the West... their knowledge of the land and their exploration of the frontier were the by-products of their search for skins and pelts. They were men who relied entirely on their instincts and sense of direction for their livelihood and survival.

The saga of the mountain men echoes with names like Kit Carson, Jim Bridger, John McBroom and Tom Tobin, men who were a hardy and fearless breed apart.

Their appearance was distinctive, too, and a true American original. Dressed in buckskin suits decorated with porcupine quills and bright beads, they sported coonskin caps that were a tradition with earlier woodsmen of the Kentucky and Tennessee hills, wore their hair braided and had leathery faces bronzed and weathered by the elements – faces much the same color as those of the Indians. In all likelihood, they smelled a little like buffalo hides drying in the sun, since they spent long winters in the woods in heavy undergarments and suits made of home-cured skins.

But the mountain men knew the lay of the land blindfolded – every nook and cranny, every canyon, boulder and pass in the region. Most of them were uneducated men, but with their sharp instincts and experience in the wilderness, they bore a complete map of the Rocky Mountains in their heads and became invaluable assets to the surveying parties of the 1850s and 60s.

For those who loved danger, the life was an exhilarating one. Indians, blizzards and freezing cold temperatures, rheumatism, exposure to the sun, and encounters with grizzly bears and rattlesnakes were routine hazards. Parched with a killing thirst, it was not uncommon to drink buffalo blood, or to drink buffalo gall mixed with water to treat illness. Facing starvation, mountain men would eat tree bark or their own moccasins if they had to.

Potentially fatal rattlesnake bites were cauterized by burning gunpowder in them, and one trapper, Thomas L. Smith, amputated his own shattered leg above the knee (it seems unkind that he was thereafter called pegleg). Jim Bridger carried an iron arrowhead in his back for years, finally having it cut out without the benefit of anesthesia. Tough hombres, wouldn't you say? And they wouldn't have survived if they hadn't been.

Nor would they have survived without ingenuity, and a tremendous amount of self-reliance and raw physical courage. The world in which they found themselves, with its vast unknown and unmarked vistas, demanded those qualities for survival but it repaid the mountain men by offering them an unparalleled sense of freedom and individualism. They traveled alone and at will, living almost entirely in the open, fearing neither Indians, animals nor hostile weather. Their wilderness skills and instinct for survival remain a part of the heritage of the Rocky Mountains.

Before the first half of the 19th century, the fur business in North America had consisted of a system of barter between Indian and white: the Indians would trap and skin the beaver and then exchange the furs for the white man's trinkets and goods, usually at trading posts that had been established for this express purpose.

In 1807, Manuel Lisa pursued the traditional method of trading, but also encouraged the men of his company to trap on their own, laying the groundwork for a new approach to the Rockies' fur trade, the brigade system.

In 1822, William H. Ashley ran the following announcement in the *Missouri Republican*:

"TO ENTERPRISING YOUNG MEN. The subscriber wishes to engage one hundred young men to ascend the Missouri River to its source, there to be employed for one, two, or three years. For particulars inquire of Major Andrew Henry, near the lead mines in the county of Washington, who will ascend with, and command, the party; or of the subscriber near St. Louis.
/s/ William H. Ashley."

Under Ashley's hand, the brigade system begun by Lisa developed into systematic trapping of most of the central Rockies and established the tradition of the "rendezvous."

The rendezvous was a trading and bartering extravaganza, where free trappers, company trappers, Indians, traders and tourists gathered once a year in a carnival atmosphere. When business was concluded – furs traded, accounts settled and supplies laid in for another winter's work – the bacchanal began! A revelry of brawling, shooting matches, horse races, gambling, boozing and sweet-talking the available ladies lasted as long as the participants could hold out – a week or sometimes longer.

And when the carnage was over, a trapper sometimes found that he had emptied his pockets of all he had earned from a year's worth of back-breaking work. Forced to turn to a trader for supplies and equipment on credit, he not only found himself in debt, but had to pledge sole rights on his next year's catch to the trader.

But that didn't stop him from coming back the next year and celebrating just as robustly – after all, a year in the wilderness was a year in the wilderness, and he had to let off steam somewhere.

By 1841, the beaver trade was over: civilization was encroaching on a region that held potential for wealth other than furs; by the middle of the 1830s, the silk top hat had become fashionable and the beaver hat went out of style; the price of beaver dropped and the selective trapping that had allowed the beaver to procreate and insure new harvests of pelts had been abandoned in a frenzy of over-trapping to show the same profit and eliminate the competition.

It was only a matter of time before the effects of this self-destructive course were felt and there was nothing left to trap – and only a short time before the tradition of the trapper faded into history – his way of life and his former hunting ground a forgotten dream and a distant memory.

The Rocky Mountains were home to many kinds of dreams and they nurtured more than one type of indomitable spirit – not the least of which was that of the prospector. While the trapper was made of the stuff of fierce individuality, the prospector had unlimited hope and courage. The gold and silver that had lured Coronado had, by 1860, attracted hundreds of men to the Rockies in search of pay streaks. They were the vanguard of the thousands that were to come to seek out the mountains' mineral wealth.

The discovery of gold in California in 1848 had begun the

feverish craze. As more and more people were bitten by the "get-rich-quick" bug, the westward movement of treasure hunters willing to follow any rainbow to fulfill their dream swelled to avalanche proportions. Some of those heading westward began their prospecting in the Rockies and others, who failed to strike it rich in California, looked to the mountains for the bonanza they had not been able to find in California.

While the prospector's life often paid off in a big way, it was a lonely one, his only companion often a small burro on which the prospector packed his tent, sleeping gear, camp utensils and pick and shovel. Day in and day out, he searched the mountainside for specimens that might be pay dirt and sampled stream gravels for gold. More often than not, he went to bed weary, and dreamed of the day when he would find piles of yellow gold so great he could not carry them, that day when he would become a rich man who could buy anything his heart desired.

And many men did, indeed, make sizeable, even fabulous fortunes. But those who took part in the 1859 stampede to Pike's Peak, Colorado, were not necessarily among them.

The story of the gold found the year before in the creeks around Pike's Peak by a party of eight men spread like wildfire, and thousands of people headed out in oxcarts, covered wagons and on horseback to the newly-discovered gold fields – their slogan, "Pike's Peak or Bust," painted on their vehicles and saddles, a message of derring-do and hope.

The stampede attracted so much attention that Horace Greeley, who was then Editor of the *New York Tribune*, went out West to see what all the excitement was about. When he did write about it, it was to write of the hardship, the suffering and of the inevitable disappointment, for Pike's Peak was one of the few historic gold rushes that proved a failure.

Perhaps Pike's Peak wasn't the place for a big killing, but the gold *was* out there for the taking – if you were in the right place at the right time. By 1868, a single valley in Montana alone had yielded $30 million worth of gold from its gravels, establishing the bustling, thriving town of Virginia City.

Many adventurers were drawn West by reports of gold and some of them became very famous. George M. Pullman came to Colorado after his invention of the sleeping car that bears his name (he claimed to have modeled the car on the double-deck bunks used in mining camps). In 1864, he sold a number of his 100-foot-long claims in the Pike's Peak region at $1000 per linear foot, which gave him a solid start on the road to wealth and prosperity and the means with which to perfect his invention.

Meyer Guggenheim and several of his sons were enormously successful in the smelting and refining business. The wealth they accumulated led to distinguished philanthropic endeavors, support of aviation research and the establishment of the Guggenheim Foundation, which supports research, fine arts and literature. (New York City's Guggenheim Museum, designed by Frank Lloyd Wright, houses one of the most important collections of contemporary art in the United States.)

Even though his name may not be as well known as those of Pullman and Guggenheim, one of the most successful of these adventurers was W.S. Stratton. A carpenter by trade, he prospected on and off as a hobby. Somewhere around 1890, he found what he called a "button of gold" in the Cripple Creek district of Montana, and put Cripple Creek on the map – by 1901, when Stratton died, the Cripple Creek mining district had produced about $125 million in gold.

When you think about the dividends involved and the fact that there was no such thing as the Internal Revenue Service to tax this money at the time, you can see that W.S. Stratton must have lived mighty comfortably, if not downright high, off the hog.

Another success story, but one with a bitter ending, is that of the eccentric Horace Tabor. Tabor was a storekeeper (and Mayor and postmaster of Leadville, Colorado) who grub-staked two prospectors, supplying them with about $100 worth of food and tools in return for a right to one-third of anything they found. His gamble paid off in the millions: Tabor became the owner of a third of a multi-million dollar ore operation. And when he branched out on his own, buying and selling mines and claims, he amassed a fabulous fortune in a short time – a phenomenon that was fairly typical in these early mining days, but Tabor seemed to have a special genius for always guessing right.

He was free with his money, giving his city a fire house and a bank, building the Tabor Opera House in Leadville and then the Tabor Grand Opera House in Denver, where he tried to establish the most splendid cultural showplace in the country.

Tabor had political ambitions, too, and went on to become Lieutenant Governor of Colorado and, for a brief 30-day period, a U.S. Senator, an appointment he received through manipulation and by virtue of having poured enormous sums into the Republican political machinery.

He was a man whom women found charming, genial and devastating, and when he went to Denver as Lieutenant Governor, he cut quite a swath with the ladies. Tabor's wife preferred to remain behind in Leadville, occupying a lavish and beautifully-appointed suite at the Clarendon Hotel that reflected her husband's flamboyant style more than it did her own unassuming personality.

Though the details of their meeting in Leadville have not been preserved, Tabor was to install a second woman in the Clarendon, the beautiful divorcée who was to become his mistress and second wife – Elizabeth McCourt Doe – the legendary Baby Doe.

One of the most magnificent looking women of the era (and the subject of Douglas Stuart Moore's opera, *The Ballad of*

Baby Doe), she was petite and golden-haired, with a soft, melodious voice and a charming presence that always made an immediate impression on those meeting her. And "Baby" (a pet name given her by her first husband) certainly impressed Horace Tabor. So much so that he married her in secret before his divorce from his wife, Augusta, became final (purportedly to avoid any charges of adultery in the days just prior to his Senate appointment).

But Tabor had his heart set on a big and splendid wedding in Washington, D.C., with the President of the United States in attendance. And he got it. Even the wedding was accompanied by scandal, however.

At the insistence of Baby Doe, who was a Catholic, the marriage was performed by a priest. And when press coverage of the opulent ceremony included the information that both parties had been previously married, the officiating priest returned the license to the marriage bureau unsigned.

But the Tabors had had their moment of glory and since they had already been married in St. Louis in the secret ceremony – never mind that Tabor had still been legally married to Augusta at the time – their feathers were unruffled.

The couple lived happily for the next ten years, although Baby was not accepted in Denver society. They lived quietly and in seclusion, raising their two girls, Elizabeth and Rose Mary Echo Silver Dollar Tabor, who was born in 1889.

And then, in 1893, the bottom fell out of everything.

With the repeal of the Sherman Act (which had guaranteed the price of silver through the Treasury's purchase of several million ounces each month at a fixed price), the price of silver plummeted from a dollar and thirty cents an ounce to fifty cents an ounce in as many minutes. This fall in the value of silver brought total financial ruin to most of the silver dollar millionaires.

Even Tabor's massive fortune depended for its health on the daily profits from his mines, and now he had nothing. With most of their possessions gone, he and baby Doe hung on to one mine, the Matchless, clinging to some dim hope that it would once again bring them millions when silver came back into its own. But they never lived to see that day.

Horace Tabor died in 1899 at the age of 71 – the postmaster of Denver, earning a mere $3000 a year. And Baby Doe died in 1935 in a shanty above the Matchless mine, a sad and lonely figure who had guarded it with a gun during the last years of her life – protecting it against intruders who might steal her dream.

When neighbors who had not seen her for several weeks broke into the cabin, they found a tragic sight, for the once magnificent woman who had so captivated Horace Tabor had frozen to death.

Turning from the sad tale of the Tabors, one of the greatest and most amusing Rocky Mountain stories is that of the diamond swindle of 1872, the year when two broken-down and weather-beaten prospectors took a long-shot on the gullibility and greed of their fellow human beings, and almost pulled off one of the most incredible scams of all time.

The prospectors, Arnold and Slack, appeared at the Bank of California one day to deposit $125,000 worth of uncut diamonds and rubies that they said they had found in "a desert portion of the West." They would say nothing more, protecting a find that was obviously worth a fortune.

Well, it didn't take long before the bank president contacted London, and it wasn't very long after that that Baron Rothschild was expressing interest in the great diamond discovery the two men had made in the United States.

Arnold and Slack finally agreed to lead a group to their claim, with the one stipulation that the men be blindfolded on the last leg of the trip and again on leaving the site of the claim. Those who went found a number of diamonds and also brought back emeralds, sapphires, rubies and amethysts.

Wealthy San Francisco investors interested in gaining control of the diamond discovery sent a mining engineer to examine the area. This time, Slack and Arnold led the engineer and his party through a circuitous route to keep the exact location secret. Following his examination (during which the two prospectors allowed him to "find" diamonds), the engineer's report recommended to the investors that they purchase the claim for $4 million. The businessmen didn't let any grass grow under their feet, and raised $2 million of the money immediately.

But the sensational story of the discovery of diamonds had piqued the curiosity of a lot of people. And when a group of U.S. geologists, led by Clarence King, visited the locality of the find, combing the soil and making tests, they found many diamond fragments that had been cut artificially. Like bloodhounds on the trace of a fresh scent, they covered every foot of the area where Arnold and Slack had staked their claim. They found that the soil had been worked over and diamonds placed at or near the surface, while other gems had been generously scattered over the entire area. It was a find all right... a real eye-opener!

It seems that the two scoundrels had "salted" their claim with about $35,000 worth of gems – including over $8,000 in "waste" material bought from a London diamond cutter – to fleece unsuspecting, but money-hungry, investors and make a fortune.

When the swindle was fully aired, the investors were repaid their $2 million, and Arnold, who was charged with fraud, had to make some minor restitutions to the complainants. But when all was said and done, he was something of a hero to his townspeople, perhaps because of the audaciousness of the sting he and Slack had tried to pull off. It was the bank president who got the worst of it in the end: *he* had purchased the worthless property on which the two prospectors had staked their bogus claim – and Baron Rothschild was no longer the least bit interested in it!

With all the discoveries and fortunes being made, and with so many mining towns striking it rich, the new wealth showed itself in grandiose and lavishly-decorated public buildings, homes and hotels. And Leadville was not to be surprised.

In 1895, around Christmas time, a spectacular building opened to the public that housed a ballroom, dining hall, riding gallery, skating rink, carousel and toboggan slide, as well as facilities for ice yachting and sleighing. Nothing special, you say? Well, read on. This was no ordinary edifice, for, with the exception of a few roof trestles, the whole building was composed of blocks of ice! The *pièce de résistance* of Leadville's massive crystal palace, which was built in Norman-style architecture, was an ice-carving of the figure of a woman of Amazon proportions. Standing nineteen feet high and resting on a pedestal of ice twenty feet square, the figure, entitled "Leadville," dominated the main entrance of the fantastic structure, which was a symbol of the kind of madness that sudden wealth can bring.

The Hotel de Paris, in Georgetown, Colorado, was owned and operated by Louis Dupuy, an outstanding chef who prided himself on the fact that the cuisine at his hotel rivaled that of any in the country. Patrons who failed to enjoy a soufflé from his kitchen or a fine wine from his cellar were simply asked to leave the premises.

And when President Ulysses S. Grant visited the Teller House in Central City, a pathway of silver bricks worth $12,000 was laid for him to walk on.

Opulence, grandeur, lavish settings and fine trappings were the boast of wealth. When the Beaumont Hotel opened in 1886 in Ouray, Colorado, it was the first hotel in the United States with alternating current; the Hotel Jerome in Aspen had an elevator that was operated by hand-pulled ropes. And Piper's Opera House in Virginia City, Nevada, was a sumptuous hall whose stage was graced by such luminaries as Enrico Caruso, Lillian Russell and the Barrymores.

But despite many such attempts at gentility, the West was still wide open, and many mining towns were rough and roaring places that attracted an amazing assortment of characters of questionable repute – mining sharks, dance-hall girls, gamblers and con-artists – all contributing their own particular shady colors to the scene.

There was no lack of excitement: outlaws preyed on banks and trains – the fame of such legends as Frank and Jesse James, the Daltons and the Younger Brothers spread far and wide, the story of their deeds told and retold by a public that glorified their daring crimes.

And there were women who were about as far from being retiring wallflowers as you can get: Calamity Jane, a tobacco-chewing bawd; Belle Starr, who carried a six-gun on either hip; and Cattle Annie McDougal and Jennie Metcalf (also known as Little Britches), who started out Bootlegging whiskey to the Indians and switched to cattle rustling when they decided on a career change.

The cattle business had begun routinely in the West as an adjunct to the great westward trek, first providing stock for hauling heavily-loaded carts and wagons and then providing beef to a growing population created by mining and its ancillary industries. With the growing demand for beef in the urbanized East and the access to slaughterhouses in Chicago and Kansas City that the railroads provided by 1867, the open-range cattle business evolved into a thriving, money-making enterprise that attracted both adventurers and investment seekers.

And it created the cowboy, a giant in the American scenario of heroic figures and the subject of never-ending fascination in films and literature. He, too, was a frontiersman, living life in the open, camping out for weeks at a time away from the home ranch, roping cattle, branding calves, breaking broncos, and relying on his stamina and endurance – because there were lots of long weeks when he had to get by with only three hours sleep a night.

The cowboy's lifestyle was one of extremes. During the winter, when all activity stopped, there was intense monotony and boredom, while the fever-pitch activity of the summer made intense physical and psychological demands. For the working season on a ranch lasted as long as the good weather held up, and the summer months had to be made the most of.

Normally, cattle had to be rounded up twice a year – in the spring and in the fall. Because there were no fences, stock wandered and mixed and had to be gathered on the open range, separated by owner and branded, dehorned, castrated and given medical attention as necessary. At the end of a succession of long, hot, dusty and exhausting days, the cowboys either returned stock to the range or moved them for shipment. The roundup process often lasted for weeks, and the summer between roundups was another tedious period of herding and loading cattle for shipment.

But the roundups of early days were also big social occasions – gatherings of people from widely-scattered ranches for celebrations that featured broncobusting, horse races, roping and branding and all manner of contests. These old-time roundups were the precursors of the modern rodeos and the Wild West shows that still travel over the country, albeit with more than an added touch of glitter and showmanship.

By the 1870s, the need for food had become so great in the British Isles that England had become the leading consumer of western beef. The extent of this trade and the enormity of American cattle operations attracted British investors who saw the opportunity for lucrative profit on the horizon. By about 1882, fifteen British companies were involved in cattle-ranching operations and the shipment of millions of dollars worth of beef to England.

And the presence of these companies had its own impact on the culture of the Rocky Mountains. In 1883, British members of the Cheyenne Club in Cheyenne, Wyoming, attended a formal, white-tie dinner where forty-one guests consumed a sumptuously prepared meal and washed it down with no less than sixty-six bottles of champagne and twenty bottles of sparkling red wine.

The great English ranch houses were another affair, equipped with all the trappings of genteel living. Their occupants were attended by butlers and maids, their gala suppers were held in the warm glow of candlelight – the tables set with delicate linens, gleaming silver and fine china, the strains of Viennese music provided by string orchestras adding a final touch to the elegant ambiance. For a brief period, not only Cheyenne, but Denver as well, showed signs of English influence, and traces of English culture are still apparent in architecture, names and traditions.

The winter of 1886-87, the winter of the "Big Die," sounded the death knell for the open-range cattle industry. Two dry summers had cut back the availability of good grazing land, and ranchers also faced the problem of low prices that prevented them from selling excess stock, further straining the already over-burdened grasslands.

When winter came, the cattle were lean and ill-prepared for harsh weather, and no hay had been stored for feed. A devastating blizzard drove starving cattle before the storm until they drifted towards fences or wire, where they huddled to die. When spring came, only a few pathetic animals per hundred were left, all ribs and skin, their feet and tails frozen. As much as seventy-five percent of the stock had died, the tragic victims of callous and unfeeling stupidity.

But even before this catastrophe occurred, more and more ranchers had begun to fence in their ranges, and open-range ranching had begun to retreat. The natural system, where cattle and men ran free, has for the most part disappeared (Wyoming is still legally an open-range state), but the cowboy has not. He can still be found – in the movies or in real life – wearing his boots and spurs and hat and, occasionally, riding off into the sunset... just like John Wayne did.

The early bonanzas of the Rocky Mountains – fur trapping, mining, farming, timber, transportation and sheep and cattle ranching – had built a large population that filled the land and consumed the resources that had once seemed endless. Gradually, the frontier began to recede, taking with it the opportunity for entrepreneurism, bonanza and profit. The land that had been at once generous, harsh and hostile had now become stingy because so many of its resources had been extracted. In a cycle of rise and decline, Rocky Mountain history was characterized by a prosperity that consumed itself. And the discovery of oil in 1862 supplied yet another material for extraction.

But the region, while repeating its old boom-and-bust patterns, was becoming increasingly aware of the need to work towards permanence. New developments in irrigation began to ensure reliable agriculture, attention turned to balanced grazing and better land management, and conservation efforts emphasized the need to nurture natural resources. The future of the Rocky Mountains depended, to a large extent, on finding ways of making a reliable living from the land without depleting its riches – building stable agricultural, grazing and forestry systems and cultivating renewable materials.

The achievement of these ends was due, to a large extent, to the federal government's involvement in directing and supporting these efforts. Under the administration of Teddy Roosevelt, an ardent conservationist, water-power sites and land (including 141 million acres designated as forest reserve) were withdrawn, and guidelines established for their use, laying the basis for a permanent public domain and, at the same time, giving the government an effective and powerful lever for controlling land and resource use.

Ultimately, federally-controlled land, including forests, parks and Indian reservations, would amount to 40 percent in Wyoming, 36 percent in Colorado and 30 percent in Montana. Grazing, timber-cutting and mineral rights are offered – either for sale or for lease – with the hope that the resources will be used wisely and productively, leaving a heritage for all to enjoy in perpetuity.

At the end of the 19th century, people began coming to the Rockies just to see the sights – to get away, to play and to be cured. Many of those who came suffered from a variety of illnesses, including tuberculosis, and it was thought that the air and the climate would cure what ailed them. (At the time, it was estimated that tuberculosis took the life of one out of ten Americans.)

Both the ailing and the healthy flocked to the Rocky Mountain resorts, which offered lavish and opulent accommodations, attracting a monied and sophisticated clientele. The resort towns boomed for twenty years, luxuriating in success. At the turn of the century, however, the German physician and bacteriologist Robert Koch made the discovery that tuberculosis was a contagious disease. When this information became known to the general public, the wealthy patrons who had infused the Rocky Mountain resorts with capital boycotted them.

Most of the resorts closed their doors, and the few that remained open lost their former luster. But, for the first time, transients of a different kind had come to the land – they had not taken its wealth and moved on; they had, instead, left their wealth behind. And it seemed that a new era had dawned, one in which yet another profitable venture beckoned on the horizon – the goldmine called tourism.

And, when you go there, you will see for yourself why the grand and magnificent scenery continues to draw visitors to the area year after year; why the region has been an inspiration to so many painters, poets, photographers and composers; and why so many people who live there find the quality of life in the Rocky Mountains exactly to their liking.

Wyoming all by itself is enough reason to visit the Rockies. It is a state famous for the beauty of its mountains, which provide the setting for the splendor of Yellowstone National Park – the nation's largest and the world's oldest national park. John Colter, who had been a member of the Lewis and Clark expedition, was probably the first white man to see Yellowstone when he traveled alone on foot through the area in 1807 and had the rare privilege of coming upon Yellowstone's deep canyons, thundering waterfalls, sparkling lakes and great expanses of evergreen forest.

Most of Yellowstone was formed by volcanic eruptions that took place over 60,000 years ago in a series of violent explosions. The park today has more geysers and hot springs than any other in the world... and the most famous geyser of all is Old Faithful, which erupts on average every sixty-five minutes, sending a stream of boiling water more that 100 feet into the air.

The park, which covers more that 2 million acres of land, is home to more than 200 species of birds and over 40 kinds of other animals, including about 1,000 bison and approximately 20,000 elk that live there in the summertime. When winter comes, the snow sculpts Yellowstone into a frosted masterpiece and the temperatures can reach as low as 65°F below zero. About half the elk will leave Yellowstone for warmer areas, and those that stay behind tough out sometimes brutal winters in a wonderland carpeted by snow – when Old Faithful plays to a virtually empty house.

Another Wyoming scenic wonder that is not to be missed is Grand Teton National Park, which includes some of the West's most beautiful mountains. The sight of the majestic Tetons rising sharply from the floor of the beautiful valley called Jackson Hole is unbelievably breathtaking. The scenic peaks, painted in the softest hues of violet, turquoise, blue and glistening white, rise nearly straight up for more than a mile. Each year, more that 8,000 elk winter beneath their colossal majesty.

Wyoming is a state of firsts: the first national park – Yellowstone; the first national monument in the country – Devil's Tower; and the first national forest – Shoshone. Nicknamed "The Equality State," Wyoming was the first state in the nation where women could vote, hold public office and serve on juries. In 1870, Wyoming's Esther H. Morris became the country's first woman justice of the peace, and in 1924 Wyoming voters elected the first woman governor, Nellie Tayloe Ross (she later became the first woman director of the U.S. Mint).

And though the natural wonders of Grand Teton National Park and Yellowstone Park alone attract several million visitors a year, it is hard to resist the lure of Arizona's Grand Canyon, a giant gorge 217 miles long and a mile or more deep. Here, perspectives shift by the hour as shadow and light play off the Canyon's myriad colors and rock formations. Forests of stately ponderosa pine sweep southward from the canyon's edge toward the 12,000-foot San Francisco Peaks, where Hopi and Navajo gods are said to dwell. Placid lakes and meadows add further to the enchantment.

And there is the magnificence of the Painted Desert, which extends about 200 miles along the Little Colorado River in northern Arizona. It is an especially brilliant sight at sunset, when fiery russet and mauve tones mix to enhance the already colorful rock and sand of the desert. Within the multi-colored Painted Desert in Petrified Forest National Park, where petrified remains of prehistoric trees (some as long as 250 feet) that were buried in mud, sand or volcanic ash lie in stony silence. The undecoded ancient Indian carvings of Newspaper Rock in Petrified Forest carry their own mysterious silence and perhaps some day will yield up their secret.

Colorado is another state blessed with unusual natural beauty. It is named for the Spanish word meaning "colored red," which was first used to describe the Colorado River winding its way through canyons of red stone. Colorado's cool, pleasant climate makes it an extremely popular center for summer visitors, and, in the winter, thousands upon thousands of skiers are attracted to the slopes of its world-famous ski resorts. The lure is no longer gold and silver... it's the powdery snow at Vail, Aspen, Estes Park and Wolf Creek.

Visitors are also drawn to Colorado by the splendor of its sights. From the delicate symmetry of its State Flower, the Rocky Mountain Columbine (look, but don't touch – the fine for picking *any* wild flower in Colorado can be $300!) to the awesome beauty of Royal Gorge, Colorado is filled with dazzling natural wonders. Among the most impressive sights are the stark sandscapes of Grand Sand Dunes National Monument, and the 250-million-year-old Garden of the Gods, a 700-acre spread near Colorado Springs studded with huge masses of red sandstone rocks. Formations in the Garden of the Gods have acquired their own names over the years because of their distinctive shapes: there is Vulcan's Anvil; the delicate Three Graces; The Balanced Rock; and, a forlorn pair, The Two Old Maids.

Colorado also offers the incredible vista from the summit of Pike's Peak. Extending for more than 100 miles, the view is so splendidly breathtaking that in 1893 it inspired Katherine Lee Bates to compose what could be, but isn't, the national anthem: "America the Beautiful."

Like Colorado, Nevada's ski slopes attract thousands of ski enthusiasts each year – and it is famous for its beautiful and serene lakes. Lake Tahoe, nestled in a valley in the rugged Sierra Nevadas, is a particularly lovely spot for enjoying the sun and swimming to your heart's content, surrounded by nature at her best. Another popular resort, Lake Mead, is a man-made lake and is the only lake in Nevada with an outlet to the sea.

But Nevada is perhaps best known for the colorful night life and gambling casinos of Las Vegas and Reno (where thousands flock for quick and easy divorces). Some of the casinos never close, and breakfast is available 24 hours a day to acccommodate a variety of gambling schedules!

When spring comes to Nevada it brings a special

enchantment – meadows bloom with Indian paintbrush, larkspur, shooting stars and violets; the blood-red blossoms of the snow plant push through the snow in the pine forests; and wild peach blossoms and desert lilies brighten Nevada's foothills. It's a particularly beautiful time for a visit... but then, anytime of the year is.

And then there is the enchantment of New Mexico. It's called "The Land of Enchantment." Filled with drama and mystery and magic, it is a land ancient in history and its earth takes varied and powerful forms. New Mexico is where the Southwest began, and where the Indian, Spanish and American West cultures both partake of each other and survive as distinct patterns. A mighty sweep of land that begins in the east with a high plain (the *llano*), swells to a great wave of forested mountains and breaks to the west in a sea of bold mesas – this is the drama of New Mexico. It is the home of the Pueblo Indians, whose ancestors were the Anasazi, the "Ancient Ones," who abandoned their cliff-dwelling homes sometime in the 14th century. The mighty Rio Grande River flows through New Mexico, running like a backbone through the state, providing the prime source of water and a fabulous and overwhelming feast for the eyes.

The famous light of New Mexico illuminates all it touches, bathing mountain, plain, desert, mesa and forest in a glow that enchants the beholder.

White Sands National Monument, the canyonscape around Angel Peak, the quiet beauty of Eagle Nest Lake, the dramatic formations of stalactites and stalagmites in Carlsbad Caverns, the beauty of the Gila Wilderness and the fascination of the Puyé Cliff dwellings are just some of the rewards of New Mexico's superb scenery.

Montana is the state where Custer fought his last stand, at Little Bighorn, and where a main street called Last Chance Gulch can be found in the capital of Helena.

The waters of Montana, born in snowmelt atop the Continental Divide, are a necklace of turquoise lakes, each placidly reflecting the image of the mountain towering above it. Its colossal Glacier National Park is the work of millions of years of the sculpting and molding forces of the giant glaciers, and many of the peaks in Glacier are so steep that they have never been climbed. The park boasts more than fifty glaciers lying on its mountain slopes, offering some of the most magnificent mountain scenery in the land. Mountaintop boardwalks make hiking in this park an easy and pleasant way to see its attractions, as do miles and miles of hiking trails.

Montana's Giant Springs is one of the largest fresh water springs in the world. Discovered in 1805 by the Lewis and Clark expedition, this extraordinary natural wonder discharges water at the rate of 338 million gallons a day.

Medicine Rocks, in the badlands of eastern Montana, was once a place of "Big Medicine," where Indian hunting parties went to conjure up magical spirits. The soft sandstone rocks, weathered by the forces of wind, water and erosion, resemble Swiss cheese. The 160-acre park at Medicine Rocks is a haven for wildlife and a popular place for campers and picnickers to enjoy the outdoors.

To most people, Montana is a place for relaxation – for fishing, hiking, water sports (including white water rafting), camping or just looking at the sights. To others, the highlight of a visit to the state might just be the big "Whoop-Up Days" held in Conrad, Montana during the month of May. If you happen to be in the area at that time of year, stop on by.

Idaho's land of canyons, high mountains clothed in pine, and green velvet vistas stretching as far as the eye can see, will soothe a tired spirit anytime. One of the country's premier wildernesses, its high mountains, moving waters and abundance of wildlife offer all the enchantment of quiet and natural surroundings. Idaho even has several primitive areas that the U.S. Forest Service has preserved without roads, logging developments or modern improvements. These can be explored only on foot, by horseback, in boats or from planes, and the reward is a first-hand look at true virgin wilderness.

Idaho has hundreds of underground caves. Its Crystal Ice Cave, near American Falls, boasts a frozen river and a frozen waterfall. Minnetonka Cave has huge chambers that look like elaborate Gothic halls, and the Shoshone Ice Caves, which lie under lava fields, have ice-covered ceilings and walls.

Weird rock formations that resemble towers, cathedrals and castles compose the Cities of Rock – all the painstaking work of nature's carving and sculpting techniques.

Idaho's Hells Canyon is the deepest in the country. Located on the Snake River, about 100 miles south of Lewiston, the canyon dramatically drops 7,900 feet at its deepest and has an average depth of about one mile.

The Shoshone Falls are truly spectacular to behold. The 212 foot waterfall in the Snake River Canyon is 52 feet higher than Niagara Falls and plunges turbulently over a horseshoe-shaped rim – not a sight you see every day.

Like Montana, Idaho shares part of Yellowstone Park with Wyoming (although most of Yellowstone lies within the State of Wyoming), and this vast expanse only increases the availability of magnificent scenery.

Idaho has many mountains of extraordinary beauty, including the Bitterroot Range, which lies on the Idaho/Montana border, and the Salmon River Mountains, which include the stunning Bighorn Crags – rough, bare mountains of granite that have been worn into sharp ridges and spires, making them among the most rugged mountains in the entire Northwest. The Sawtooth Mountains, rising south of the Salmon River, are the state's most beautiful, with lovely lakes and exquisitely-colored meadows. (The Salmon River is called "The River of No Return," because travelers once could not navigate upstream against its furious current and treacherous rapids).

Southern Idaho has more than 100 mineral springs. Among the most famous is Warm Springs, near Boise. The waters there have a temperature of 170°F, and are even piped into some Boise homes to provide heat.

Idaho is the perfect place for those who love lakes, because it has more than 2,000 – with several hundred more still to be explored (these are lakes that have only been seen from planes). Pend Oreille Lake and Lake Coeur D'Alene are two of the most beautiful, as entrancing as the poetical sound of their names.

And, of course, there is one of Idaho's least-kept secrets – Sun Valley – where skiers enjoy the sun, the air, the camaraderie and the thrill of the slopes.

But there is one more thing about Idaho that simply cannot be overlooked: the Idaho potato. There are few things in life more mouth-watering to the palate than the taste of a baked Idaho, served hot from the oven with a dash of salt and pepper and a healthy serving of butter. Pure heaven!

Nature has been as generous to Utah as it has to the other Rocky Mountain states. Snow-covered mountains, multi-colored canyons and beautiful forests, lakes and rivers create Utah's landscape. Deserts cover about one-third of the state, and few plants can grow there because of the lack of rainfall. Utah's rivers are used to provide irrigation for farmlands that would otherwise be desert. Rich in mineral deposits, Utah is the location of the Bingham Canyon Copper Pit (the largest open-pit copper mine in all of North America), which produces about a seventh of the nation's copper. The discovery of uranium in 1952 near Moab set off a "uranium rush" that echoed the frenzied gold rush of a century before.

In 1847, Brigham Young and the first Mormon pioneers arrived in the Great Salt Lake region of Utah, establishing the State of Deseret two years later. Deseret is a Mormon word meaning honeybee, and represents the ideals of industry and hard work. When Utah was organized as a territory by Congress in 1850, it was named after the Ute Indian tribe that lived there. The Mormon tradition continues, however, in Utah's nickname – "The Beehive State." Today, Mormons make up more than seventy percent of Utah's population.

The Mormon presence is especially evident in Salt Lake City, the headquarters of the Church of Jesus Christ of Latter Day Saints, where Temple Square houses the majestically-spired Mormon Temple – a structure that took 40 years to build. The famous Salt Lake Tabernacle, with its huge organ and world-renowned Mormon Tabernacle Choir, is here. The Choir's live performances, as well as its recordings, thrill millions of listeners each year.

Temple Square is also the site of Seagull Monument, built as a tribute to the gulls from Great Salt Lake that saved Utah's crops in 1848 from the swarms of grasshoppers that later became known as Mormon crickets.

Thousands of years ago, parts of Utah were covered by a vast body of fresh water, an ancient sea that scientists have named Lake Bonneville. Today, the Bonneville Salt Flats, in the middle of Great Salt Lake Desert, cover part of Lake Bonneville's bed. Great Salt Lake and Utah Lake are also part of what remains of Lake Bonneville. Great Salt Lake is quite phenomenal. It is the largest natural lake west of the Mississippi, and because it is from four to seven times as salty an any ocean, swimmers can float in its waters with the greatest of ease – without fear of sinking.

Great Salt Lake Desert has about 4,000 acres of flat salt beds that are as hard as concrete. The hot, dry climate causes stark cracks in the desert and makes it one of the most desolate spots anywhere. Stretching over the hard salt beds is the Bonneville Speedway, where, in 1947, a British driver named John Cobb was the first to travel at more than 400 miles an hour on land.

At scenic Monument Valley, a Navajo tribal park, there are red sandstone formations that rise 100 feet into the air and, in the evening, a formation called the "totem pole" casts an eerie shadow that stretches for miles.

Utah has five national parks: Arches, Bryce Canyon, Canyonlands, Capitol Reef and Zion. Bryce Canyon is a symphony of brilliant color, and in Zion National Park the massive, stony shapes of Great White Throne rise nearly half a mile from the canyon floor. Zion Canyon is a particularly spectacular example of river erosion.

The Wasatch Mountains offer wonderful skiing, and Utah's siren call can be heard in the Uinta Mountains, where Bear River, fed by melting snow, offers some of the best fishing anywhere – in a setting fit for the gods.

And that's what the Rocky Mountains are – fit for the gods. Or, perhaps, created by them for their own pleasure. And as for us, if we are wise we will etch every line of that magnificent land in our memories and treasure what he have been privileged to see. For as the Navajos say... everything forgotten returns to the circling winds.

Previous page: Hunter Peak is among the highest of the Guadalupe Mountains, which rise above the Texas plains to form the southernmost end of the Rocky Mountain Range. Groundwater, percolating through an ancient limestone reef, created the strange rock formations of the Carlsbad Caverns (these pages), beneath the foothills of the Guadalupe Mountains in New Mexico.

Above: Monument Canyon, Colorado, with the pale Book Cliff Mountains in the distance. Facing page: the sandstone cliffs of the Mesa Verde. Overleaf: (right) the Cliff Palace in Mesa Verde National Park, Colorado, was built by Pueblo Indians towards the end of the 12th century. (Left) the violence of an electric storm over the Mesa Verde.

Above: scrub-covered San Luis Valley, and (facing page) the Great Sand Dunes National Monument, which extends for ten miles below the Sangre de Cristo Range's western slopes. Overleaf: (left) the spectacular Rio Grande flows through the Creede area. (Right) reflections in Cottonwood Lake, in San Isabel National Forest.

Facing page: the Cimarron Creek weaves its way northward towards the Gunnison River.
Above: Red Mountain, in the San Juan Range, caught in the light of the setting sun.
Overleaf: the snow-dusted peaks of the San Juan Mountains around Telluride.

These pages: evening light in the town of Telluride, surrounded by the massive peaks and harsh cliffs of the San Juan Mountains. Overleaf: (left) Telluride viewed from the ore-rich slopes which triggered its existence in the 1870s, when gold and silver strikes attracted prospectors to build a rough, colorful mining town. (Right) forested slopes above the town.

Above: the brightly-painted houses of Telluride, and (facing page) Colorado Avenue, the town's main street, where many of the original Victorian buildings have been carefully restored. Overleaf: views of Telluride, which was first incorporated in 1875 as the town of Columbia. It was rechristened a few years later, the new name deriving from a type of silver and gold ore found in the presence of tellurium.

Above and overleaf, left: Telluride has developed as a successful ski-resort, the slopes above the Victorian town offering some of the finest expert skiing in Colorado. Facing page: Colorado Avenue at dusk, and (overleaf, right) the town spread out along the narrow valley of the San Miguel River.

Above: deep snow covers the folds of the San Juan Mountains, and (facing page) lies in the San Miguel River Valley. Overleaf: (left) skiers at the base of a Telluride ski-run, and (right) the cathedral-like walls of Black Canyon, cut by the waters of the Gunnison River.

Above: Imogen Pass, and (facing page) Engineers Pass, in the Ouray area, whose snow-capped peaks and green valleys have earned it the title "The Switzerland of America." Overleaf: (left) gray scree slopes in Imogen Pass, and (right) summer in a valley of the Western Rockies.

Steep-sided mountains dotted with old mine workings encompass the town of Ouray (these pages). Named after the peacemaking chieftain of the Southern Utes, Ouray stands on ground that was considered sacred by the Indians. Overleaf: the debris of long-exhausted mines still litters the ghost town of Tomboy, on the Imogen Pass.

Facing page: a green Alpine valley in the Ouray area, and (above) flat pastureland below
the jagged Sneffels Range, near Ridgeway. Overleaf: snow in the mountains, near the town
of Ridgeway.

Above: a freezing river, near Ridgeway, and (facing page) sun on the Rocky Mountains, seen from Highway 62 as the road passes near the town. Overleaf: (left) a saloon, and (right) small stores, in the mountain town of Ridgeway.

Previous page: (left) wooded foothills near Colona, and (right) Mount Sneffels, which rises to a height of 14,143 feet. These pages: the peaks of the magnificent Sawatch Range, which includes some of Colorado's highest mountains, drop steeply to the waters of the Twin Lakes. Overleaf: (left) reflections in Dream Lake, and (right) aspen- and conifer-covered slopes in Gunnison National Forest.

Skiing in the Monarch Ski Area, (above) at the top of the Breeze Way Lift, and (facing page) on the great ridge at the top of Panorama Lift. This fine ski area is situated on Monarch Pass, in a particularly high section of Colorado's Central Rockies, and forms part of the continental watershed, separating the Arkansas River Valley to the east from the Gunnison River Valley to the west.

Previous pages: (left) skiing down Breeze Way run, and (right) Garfield run, in the
Monarch Ski Area. These pages and overleaf: magnificent views towards Chair Mountain, near
8,755-foot-high McClure Pass, White River National Forest.

Aptly named Crystal River (above) winds between thickly wooded banks, near the town of Marble in White River National Forest. Facing page: contrasting woodland covers the hills around Ashcroft, near Aspen. Overleaf: (left) Shallow Creek Lake, on a tributary of the Rio Grande, and (right) McKee Pond, near the town of Marble.

The ski mountain at Snowmass Ski Area (these pages) is the third largest in North America, and offers fine skiing on, for example, the famous, broad mountain face of Big Burn. Overleaf: relaxing in Snowmass Ski Village, which has been developed particularly as a family resort.

Previous pages: vacationers in Snowmass Ski Village. Facing page: the greens and golds of fir and aspen trees edge Bear Lake, in Rocky Mountain National Park. Above: Colorado's famed Maroon Bells, part of the Elk Range, overlook the waters of Maroon Lake in the brilliant sunshine of an Indian summer. Overleaf: (left) Hidden Valley, and (right) Maroon Creek winding towards Aspen.

Above: skiing at the top of Olympic Lift, and (facing page) looking down into the valley from Aspen Highlands, one of the four ski mountains within reach of the glamorous ski resort of Aspen.
Overleaf: looking west to clouded peaks from Olympic Lift, Aspen Highlands.

These pages: viewed from the top of Loges Peak Lift, mountain streams score the steep slopes around Aspen Highlands. Loges Peak Lift carries skiers to the more difficult trails at the top of the mountain, to which the lift-served vertical rise, 3,800 feet, is the highest in Colorado. Overleaf: (left) dark forests, and (right) Highlands Bowl, seen from the top of Loges Peak Lift.

Above: skiers compete in the freestyle contest, held throughout the season near the Merry-Go-Round Restaurant on Aspen Highlands. Facing page: the high ridges of the Rockies stretch away from Aspen Highlands. Overleaf: ski-jumping, part of the freestyle competitions.

Spectacular ski-jumping (above) in the freestyle contest outside the Merry-Go-Round Restaurant, and (facing page and overleaf) higher up the mountain at the top of Cloud 9 Lift. Here, members of the Aspen Highlands Ski Patrol provide a daily display of aerobatics, ski-jumping over the sun deck by the Cloud 9 Restaurant.

Above: skiers spectating near Thunderbowl Lift, on Aspen Highlands, and (facing page) relaxing at the Merry-Go-Round Restaurant. Overleaf: (left) view near Broadway run, at the top of Aspen Highlands and (right) the crest of Highlands Peak above its huge powder bowl, where only expert skiers venture, under guidance from the ski patrol.

Above: ski run on Aspen Mountain, a demanding mountain providing good intermediate and advanced skiing.
In contrast, Buttermilk Mountain (facing page) is Aspen Ski Area's teaching mountain, offering gentler
gradients for first-time skiers. Overleaf: (left) Little Nell Lift, on Aspen Mountain (right).

Above: Cooper Avenue, in the town of Aspen, and (facing page) Cooper Street Mall, with Aspen Mountain beyond. Overleaf: twilight (left) in Durant Avenue, outside Little Nell's cafe at the base of Aspen Mountain, and (right) in Hyman Avenue Mall.

Aspen is Colorado's quintessential ski resort town, where the atmosphere of the small, Victorian mountain community exists alongside the glamour of a resort frequented by the rich and famous. Above: Aspen town center, and (facing page) Hopkins Avenue, Aspen. Overleaf: (left) the town's shopping center, and (right) Galena Street at night.

Previous page: (left) Christmas in Aspen's shopping center, and (right) traditional transport available in Galena Street. Above: golden aspens line the banks of Crystal Creek, in Gunnison National Forest, and (facing page) blanket the land around Independence Pass.

Previous page: (left) Maroon Creek, which flows through the mountains to meet the Roaring Fork River at
Aspen, and (right) the clear waters of Maroon Lake. East of Aspen lies the town of Leadville (above),
once the world's greatest silver camp, from which Highway 24 now winds through the Rockies (facing page).

Above: Breckenridge town and Ski Area, seen from Boreas Pass road, and (facing page) the town at dusk. Overleaf: Breckenridge (left) began life as a rough mining town when the Blue River Valley was discovered by gold prospectors in 1859. In recent years the town has developed rapidly as a resort, offering fine skiing on Peaks 8 and 9 (right).

Above: skating in Breckenridge Ski Village, and (facing page) forests of skis outside Peak 8 Restaurant. Overleaf: (left) skiers at the base of D Lift, and (right) smooth peaks top the radiating ski runs of Breckenridge.

Previous page: (left) Horseshoe Bowl, and (right) the vast peaks above Breckenridge Ski Area. East of Breckenridge lies Copper Mountain Ski Area (facing page), where the U.S. Alpine Championship Men's Giant Slalom is pictured (this page and overleaf).

144

Previous pages: deep snow on Copper Mountain, among the jagged peaks of Arapaho National Park. These pages: dark forests and white peaks form a dramatic backdrop to Main Street, in the mountain town of Frisco.

Above: ski lift at Loveland Pass, in the Arapaho National Forest, and (facing page) looking north through snow-clouds over Berthoud Pass. Overleaf: (left) the view towards Keystone over 11,992-foot-high Loveland Pass, and (right) ski runs in the Arapaho Basin.

Above: roads snake away down the valley, past Vail Ski Village, and (facing page) forests
of winter aspens shade the slopes beneath Eagles Nest, on Vail's ski mountain. Overleaf:
(left) ski-tracks pattern the snow. (Right) ski runs near Wildwood ski station, Vail.

The luxury accommodation and leisure facilities of Vail Ski Village (these pages and overleaf) extend for nearly 15 miles along the narrow valley of Gore Creek. The potential of Vail Mountain as a world-class ski resort was first recognised in 1954, and the mountain and village were developed rapidly, opening in 1962.

Vail (above) is a town entirely purpose-built to offer the highest class of service to its visitors.
Colorado's biggest single ski mountain, Vail Mountain provides exhilarating skiing and spectacular views,
from Mid-Vail ski station?? (facing page and overleaf, right), and Eagle's Nest (overleaf, left).

162

Visitors to Vail display their skiing expertise and fashions in ski-wear (this page and overleaf, left). Facing page and overleaf, right: forbidding Rocky Mountain peaks, seen from the Summit of Vail Mountain.

Previous pages: the magnificence of the Rocky Mountains, viewed from Vail's Wildwood ski station. These pages: the icy Colorado River winds through gentler hills, near Bond. Overleaf: (left) State Highway 131, between Bond and Wolcott. (Right) red-brown rock strata show through the snow, near Wolcott.

Previous page: (left) farmland outside Phippsburg, in the valley of the Yampa River, and (right) cattle near Steamboat Ski Area. Above: welcoming flags fly outside Steamboat Springs, where (facing page) low cloud obscures the ski mountain. Overleaf: sunset throws a yellow light across the slopes around Steamboat.

These pages: Lincoln Avenue, the main street of the town of Steamboat Springs. Unlike Vail,
Steamboat Ski Area evolved from an already well-established town. Steamboat Springs (overleaf) is a
century-old ranching town, the commercial center of the prosperous Yampa Valley ranching community.

Facing page and overleaf, left: Stagecoach Gondola carries visitors up the mountain from Steamboat Village (left, top pictures and overleaf, right), a cluster of condominiums, shops and restaurants developed as an extension of the old town. The cowboy character of Steamboat Springs is still strong, as in Eleventh Street (above).

Above: Thunderhead Restaurant, at the top of the scenic Stagecoach Gondola ride up Steamboat mountain. **Facing page and overleaf:** Steamboat's vacationers prepare to undertake the ski runs which radiate from the 9,100-foot-high summit of Thunderhead.

194

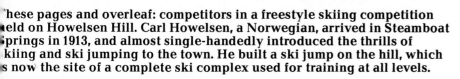
These pages and overleaf: competitors in a freestyle skiing competition held on Howelsen Hill. Carl Howelsen, a Norwegian, arrived in Steamboat Springs in 1913, and almost single-handedly introduced the thrills of skiing and ski jumping to the town. He built a ski jump on the hill, which is now the site of a complete ski complex used for training at all levels.

These pages: ski lifts carry vacationers up into Steamboat Ski Area, a huge mountain with over 1,000 skiable acres stretching across four west-facing peaks. Overleaf: (left) aspen-covered ridges seen from the top of Stagecoach Gondola and (right) Steamboat Ski Village.

Above: the towering peaks of the Mummy Range, near Deer Range Junction, Rocky Mountain National Park. At the park's eastern edge lies the popular mountain resort of Estes Park (facing page).

Above: the isolated, onion-domed Memorial Chapel, on the slopes of Peaceful Valley in Roosevelt National Forest. Further south, the famous Georgetown Loop Railroad (facing page) connects the towns of Georgetown and Silver Plume, and was first opened in 1884. Overleaf: (left) the dramatic outlines of Rocky Mountain National Park have been sculpted by millions of years of ice and wind action. (Right) Round Top Mountain.

Above: Flat-Top Mountain rises beyond Lower Green Lake, in Bridger Wilderness. Facing page: Jackson Lake, in the Grand Teton Mountains of Wyoming, lies in the deep groove left by a Piedmont glacier during the first Ice Age. Overleaf: (left) the Grand Tetons rise abruptly beyond the banks of the Snake River, Wyoming. (Right) Jenny Lake, motionless at the foot of Grand Teton and Mount Teewinot.

Above: Minerva Terrace, at Mammoth Hot Springs, Yellowstone National Park, is a beautiful terrace made of travertine, a form of calcium carbonate that has been dissolved from limestone beneath the ground and carried to the surface by hot water. Facing page: thick snow below the Grand Tetons. Overleaf: (left) Mount Moran, mirrored in the waters of Oxbow Bend, and (right) the pale silhouette of the Grand Tetons.

Above: the Lower Falls of the Yellowstone River, where the waters of the river plunge a breathtaking 308 feet, and (facing page) the Upper Falls. Overleaf: (left) raft trip along the Shoshone River, and (right) the Snake River, winding through Grand Teton National Park.

Above: Midway Geyser Basin, Wyoming, producing clouds of steam even in the cold of winter. Facing page: sunset colors the Snake River at Oxbow Bend. Overleaf: (left) bison at the aptly-named Opalescent Pool, in Black Sand Basin, Yellowstone National Park, and (right) Grand Teton, the range's highest peak.

Above: Jenny Lake, Grand Teton National Park. Facing page: the view from Logan Pass, the highest point along Going-to-the-Sun Road, in Glacier National Park, Montana. Overleaf: (left) Swiftcurrent Lake, with Grinnell Point and Gould Mountain, and (right) the sheer face of Garden Wall, towering above McDonald Creek, in Glacier National Park.

FIRE

In the valley below are three generations of forests. Can you see them?

The still, torn and bleak on the surrounding slope are testimony from the lightning-caused Glacier Wall fire that consumed over 1,000 acres in 1967.

The second and older stand of trees up the valley is regrowth from the 1936 Heaven's Peak fire, also lightning-caused that blackened 7,942 acres.

Surrounding the Heaven's Peak burn is the larger and darker growth of the oldest generation.

In a wilderness forest, naturally caused and perhaps necessary. They burn dead branches, needles and fire-resistant species under the burning heat of the passing heat begins. Open it always for the...

Sunrise gilds Mount Sinopah, beyond the shores of Two Medicine Lake (above), and jagged mountains surround St. Mary Lake and Wild Geese Island (facing page), in Glacier National Park, Montana. Overleaf: (left) the sharp peak of Fusillade Mountain, and (right) glacier lilies below Mount Clements, Glacier National Park.

Above: the Prince of Wales Hotel, in the idyllic setting of Waterton Lakes National Park. Facing page: fishing in Cameron Lake, in the Canadian section of Waterton Lakes National Park. Overleaf: (left) walking Crypt Lake Trail, and (right) golf, in Waterton Lakes National Park.

At the entrance to Waterton Lakes National Park lies Bison Paddocks (these pages), where, against the sheer backdrop of the Canadian Rockies, buffalo graze the prairie. Overleaf: (left) Blakiston Valley, seen from the Mount Crandell viewpoint, and (right) the grasslands of Alberta.

Above: the Rocky Mountains reflected in a waterhole at Twin Buttes, and (facing page) Vimy Ridge and Mount Richards, far across Maskinonge Lake, Alberta. Overleaf: (left) a stream in Red Rock Canyon, in the Blakiston Valley. (Right) Waterton Park Townsite on the shores of Upper Waterton Lake, seen from Bear's Hump Ridge.

Above: the devastation of Vermilion Fire Burn, in Kootenay National Park, British Columbia. Facing page: mirror images of Mount Harkin and the surrounding peaks, Kootenay National Park. Overleaf: (left) the boardwalk of Giant Cedars Trail winds through forest in Mount Revelstoke National Park, where (right) sunset colors the peaks.

Above: clouds move through a valley on the slopes of Mount MacDonald, and (facing page) the Asulkan Glacier and Dome Point, viewed from Alpine Meadow on Abbott Ridge, Glacier National Park. Overleaf: (left) Schaeffer Lake, surrounded by forbidding peaks, and (right) the forested slopes of Yoho National Park.

These pages: snows of autumn blanket the Mount Odaray Plateau Grand View, Yoho National Park. Overleaf: (left) the milky waters of Wapta Falls, pictured at dusk from the logging road, and (right) Lake Oesa, below mounts Lefroy and Yukness, British Columbia.

The cloudy blue waters of Peyto Lake (these pages) find their way down the mountains as meltwater from Peyto Glacier, Banff National Park. Overleaf: winter lends a fairytale quality to Moraine Lake (left), in the Valley of the Ten Peaks, and Lake Louise (right), Banff National Park.

259

Previous page: (left) deep snow in Banff National Park, Alberta, and (right) Moraine Lake, in the Valley of the Ten Peaks. One of the Rocky Mountains' most beautiful lakes, Lake Louise is pictured (above) in mid-winter and (overleaf, left) very still in early morning sunlight. Facing page: Mount Rundle reflected in the waters of Vermilion Lake, and (overleaf, right) under heavy rain clouds, in Banff National Park.

Founded in 1885, Banff (these pages) is the oldest of Canada's national parks, and incorporates more than 400 square kilometers of spectacular Rocky Mountain scenery. Overleaf: the wide Athabasca River flows northward between forested banks, in Jasper National Park.

Previous page: (left) a wary deer beside Medicine Lake, Jasper National Park, and (right) the turbulent Athabasca River. Meltwater from the Columbia Icefields (above and overleaf, right) feeds the great rivers of the plains. Facing page: seen from Mount Norquay, the town of Banff spreads across the lower slopes of Mount Rundle. Overleaf: (left) peaceful sunset over an Albertan lake.

Medicine Lake (above and previous page, left) lies in the extreme west of Alberta. Previous page, right: the Athabasca Glacier, Jasper National Park. Facing page: reflections in Maligne Lake, Jasper National Park. Overleaf: (left) Mushroom Peak and the Athabasca Valley, and (right) Medicine Lake at dawn.

Above: Angel Glacier, on the slopes of Mount Edith Cavell, caught in the first rays of sunlight. Facing page: hikers negotiate the deep crevasses of Athabasca Glacier. Overleaf: (left) the sheer-sided canyon of Maligne River, and (right) the wider valley of the Robson River, below the white peak of Mount Robson. Following page: (left) Rocky Mountain peaks near Banff, and (right) Mount Assiniboine, Alberta.

INDEX